The
COLD WAR

ENZO GEORGE

Cavendish
Square

New York

Published in 2016 by Cavendish Square Publishing, LLC
243 5th Avenue, Suite 136, New York, NY 10016

© 2016 Brown Bear Books Ltd

First Edition

Website: cavendishsq.com

This publication represents the opinions and views of the author based on his or her personal experiences, knowledge, and research. The information in this book serves as a general guide only. the author and publisher have used their best efforts in preparing this book and disclaim liability rising directly or indirectly from the use and application of this book.

CPSIA Compliance Information: Batch #WS15CSQ

All websites were available and accurate when this book was sent to press.

Library of Congress Cataloging-in-Publication Data

George, Enzo.
The Cold War / by Enzo George.
  p. cm. — (Primary sources in U.S. history)
Includes index.
ISBN 978-1-50260-498-9 (hardcover) ISBN 978-1-50260-499-6 (ebook)
1. Cold War — Juvenile literature. 2. World politics — 1945-1989 — Juvenile literature. I. George, Enzo. II. Title.
D843.G47 2016
909.82—d23

For Brown Bear Books Ltd:
Editorial Director: Lindsey Lowe
Managing Editor: Tim Cooke
Children's Publisher: Anne O'Daly
Design Manager: Keith Davis
Designer: Lynne Lennon
Picture Manager: Sophie Mortimer

Picture Credits:
Front Cover : bottom © Alamy/Barry Lewis; center right © Robert Hunt Library.
All images © Robert Hunt Library except; 42 © Alamy/DIZ Munchen GmbH; 24, 39 © Department of Defense; 23 © Dreamstime/Marcovaroo; 34, 35 © Gerald Ford Library; 6, 8, 9, 10, 25, 37 © Library of Congress; 30, 31 © NASA; 21, 32, 33, 38, 40, 41 © National Archives; 43 © New York Daily News; 27 © Newspaper Museum.

Brown Bear Books has made every attempt to contact the copyright holder.
If you have any information please contact licensing@brownbearbooks.co.uk

We believe the extracts included in this book to be material in the public domain.
Anyone having further information should contact licensing@brownbearbooks.co.uk

Manufactured in the United States of America

CONTENTS

INTRODUCTION

Primary sources are the best way to get close to people from the past. They include the things people wrote in diaries, letters, or books; the paintings, drawings, maps, or cartoons they created; and even the buildings they constructed, the clothes they wore, or the possessions they owned. Such sources often reveal a lot about how people saw themselves and how they thought about their world.

This book collects a range of primary sources from the Cold War, the name given to the period from the end of World War II (1939–1945) to the collapse of communist rule in Eastern Europe in 1989. The period was dominated by tension between the democratic United States and the communist Soviet Union and their respective allies.

As the Soviets enforced communism on its territories in postwar Eastern Europe, the U.S. became anxious. Both sides possessed nuclear weapons, which made the prospect of conflict terrifying, but U.S. and Soviet troops never directly fought one another. Instead there were military confrontations between countries supported by them, particularly in Korea (1950–1953) and Vietnam (1965–1973). Meanwhile, the battle for superiority between the United States and the Soviets expressed itself in areas such as technology.

HOW TO USE THIS BOOK

Each spread contains at least one primary source. Look out for "Source Explored" boxes that explain images from the Cold War and who made them and why. There are also "As They Saw It" boxes that contain quotes from people of the period.

Some boxes contain more detailed information about a particular aspect of a subject. The subjects are arranged in roughly chronological order. They focus on key events or people. There is a full timeline of the period at the back of the book.

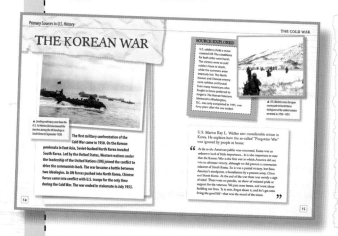

Some spreads feature a longer extract from a contemporary eyewitness. Look for the colored introduction that explains who the writer is and the origin of his or her account. These accounts are often accompanied by a related visual primary source.

USSR AND EUROPE

The end of World War II (1939–1945) left Soviet troops occupying most of Eastern Europe. The Soviets wanted the region to become a buffer between Russia and Germany, and used their influence to ensure that countries such as Hungary, Poland, and Czechoslovakia were governed according to Moscow's wishes.

Many countries became communist puppet states. Postwar Europe was divided between West and East by what was termed an "iron curtain."

▼ The Allies agreed to Soviet control of Eastern Europe at Potsdam in 1945: (left to right) new British Prime Minister Clement Attlee, President Harry S. Truman, and Soviet dictator Joseph Stalin.

SOURCE EXPLORED

Soviet tanks appeared on the streets of Budapest, Hungary, in November 1956. The Soviets had dominated politics in Eastern European countries for over a decade. They put communist governments in place that imposed strict controls on their citizens. After the death of Joseph Stalin in 1953, Hungarians wanted freedom from Soviet rule. In October 1956 there were anti-Soviet protests in Budapest and Imre Nagy became prime minister. He promised the Hungarians more freedom. The Soviets sent in one thousand tanks and also bombed Budapest from the air as the West did nothing. The Soviets crushed the Hungarian uprising as a warning to the rest of Eastern Europe.

AS THEY SAW IT

" Let us not be deceived—we are today in the midst of a cold war. Our enemies are to be found abroad and at home. Let us never forget this: Our unrest is the heart of their success. The peace of the world is the hope and the goal of our political system; it is the despair and defeat of those who stand against us. "

—Bernard Baruch, U.S. presidential advisor, uses the phrase Cold War for the first time, April 16, 1947

◀ Soviet tanks block the streets of the Hungarian capital, Budapest, on November 4, 1956.

THE UNITED STATES AND THE USSR

At the end of World War II the United States was anxious that the spread of Soviet communism would weaken its own global influence. In 1947 Harry S. Truman announced that the United States would help any country threatened by communism. The Soviets saw this Truman Doctrine as a direct threat to its influence. They were also suspicious of the U.S. Marshall Plan, which provided financial help to rebuild Europe. By the 1950s the two former Allies had become bitter opponents.

◄ *A mushroom cloud rises during U.S. nuclear tests in the Pacific in July 1946. Nuclear weapons made any conflict between the superpowers potentially disastrous.*

◄ West Berliners watch as a transport airplane comes in to land. Pilots sometimes threw candy for the children below.

SOURCE EXPLORED

Inhabitants of West Berlin watch an airplane fly in food, fuel, and other supplies during the Berlin Airlift. From June 28, 1948, until May 12, 1949, the Soviets shut off all access to West Berlin through East Germany. In the first crisis of the Cold War, the Soviet blockade aimed to make it impossible for the Western Allies to run the parts of Berlin under their control. The Americans, aided by the British and French, decided to fly in all supplies by air. During the blockade, U.S. transport aircraft flew around the clock, making almost 190,000 flights. The Soviets did not dare attack the supply planes for fear of sparking a war. When it became clear that Berlin had survived, the Soviets lifted the blockade.

MARSHALL PLAN

After the war, much of Europe was in ruins. Economies were devastated and millions of people went hungry. U.S. Secretary of State George Marshall proposed helping Europe with a program of money, food, and supplies. The aid was offered to both communist and noncommunist countries, but the Soviet Union was suspicious of U.S. influence. It turned down the offer of help on behalf of the countries under its control. The Marshall Plan even helped to drive the former allies further apart.

MUTUALLY ASSURED DESTRUCTION

▲ U.S. scientists test-fire a Minuteman Missile. The missiles were developed to carry nuclear warheads to strike at the Soviet Union.

The nuclear age began in July 1945, when U.S. scientists successfully tested an atomic bomb. By 1949 the Soviets had developed their own nuclear weapons. Any future world war now had the potential to result in the total destruction of whole countries. Both sides raced to produce more and more nuclear weapons. The theory was that they would be used only as a threat. No enemy would launch an attack if they knew it would end in what was named "mutually assured destruction" (MAD)—the extinction of both sides.

SOURCE EXPLORED

In 1962 U.S. author Chuck West wrote this handbook about how to survive a nuclear bomb in a fallout shelter. In the 1950s and 1960s many Americans feared a possible Soviet attack. Thousands of families bought or built fallout shelters. The buried shelters were lined with concrete to protect against both a nuclear blast and later radiation. Advice said that families would have to stay in a shelter for at least two weeks after a blast to avoid contamination by radioactive dust. The shelter had to be big enough for the family, their furniture, their food and water, and books and board games to while away the time until they left the shelter.

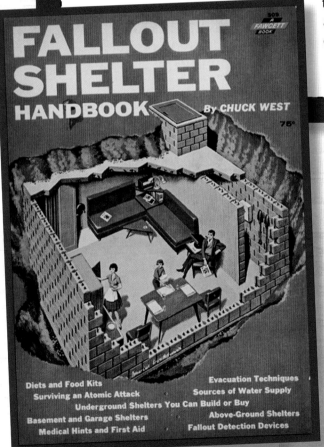

▲ The cover of West's book shows a cutaway diagram of an idealized family shelter that resembles a regular living room.

AS THEY SAW IT

" Newlyweds Mr. and Mrs. Melvin Mininson subjected their brand new marriage to the strain of 14 days [the crucial period of fallout danger] of unbroken togetherness in a twenty-two-ton steel and concrete shelter underground... The Mininsons had been hot and dusty... [but] found they could do without their fresh-air blower for six hours at a time without suffering ill effects. "

–Life magazine, August 10, 1959

THE SPACE RACE

As the United States and the Soviet Union looked for an advantage in the nuclear arms race, improving missile technology opened a new area for competition: the conquest of space. Breakthroughs in space exploration would bring international respect in addition to any improvements in technology. For much of the 1950s into the early 1960s, the Soviets led the space race. They were first to put an artificial satellite into orbit (*Sputnik I*, in 1957). They also sent the first living creature (Laika the dog, also in 1957) and the first human (Yuri Gagarin, in 1961) into space. The Americans were losing the space race.

▶ *Yuri Gagarin became famous around the world after he became the first human being in space in 1961.*

▼ *A Russian stamp celebrates the USSR space program. The Soviets gained great admiration for their achievements in space.*

AS THEY SAW IT

" From space, the masters of infinity would have the power to control the earth's weather, to cause drought and flood, to change the tides and raise the levels of the sea, to divert the gulf stream and change temperate climates to frigid... The Soviet Union has appraised control of space as a goal of such consequence that such control has been made a first aim of national policy. "

–Future president Lyndon B. Johnson argues for a U.S. space program, 1958.

SOURCE EXPLORED

This Russian stamp from 1967 commemorates Soviet successes in the space race. On April 12, 1961, the cosmonaut (Russian astronaut) Yuri Gagarin became the first man in space. A fighter pilot, Gagarin was chosen for the mission because of his broad smile, which the Soviet space director, Sergei Korolev, realized would appear in every newspaper across the globe. The 108-minute flight, during which Gagarin's spacecraft *Vostok I* orbited the Earth, was a huge propaganda victory for the Soviet Union. Gagarin became a national hero who was met with adoration wherever he went. His death in 1968, when his MiG-15 jet crashed, led to an outpouring of grief. Gagarin was given a state funeral in acknowledgment of his achievement.

THE KOREAN WAR

▲ Landing craft carry men from the U.S. 1st Marine Division toward the beaches during the UN landings in South Korea in September 1950.

The first military confrontation of the Cold War came in 1950. On the Korean peninsula in East Asia, Soviet-backed North Korea invaded South Korea. Led by the United States, Western nations under the leadership of the United Nations (UN) joined the conflict to drive the communists back. The war became a battle between two ideologies. As UN forces pushed into North Korea, Chinese forces came into conflict with U.S. troops for the only time during the Cold War. The war ended in stalemate in July 1953.

SOURCE EXPLORED

U.S. soldiers climb a snow-covered hill. The conditions for both sides were harsh. The winters were so cold soldiers froze to death, while the summers were intensely hot. The North Korean and Chinese enemies were ruthless and brutal. Even many Americans who fought in Korea preferred to forget it. The Korean Veterans Memorial in Washington, D.C., was only completed in 1995, over forty years after the war ended.

▲ *U.S. Marines cross the open countryside in North Korea during one of the coldest winters on record, in 1950–1951.*

U.S. Marine Ray L. Walker saw considerable action in Korea. He explains how the so-called "Forgotten War" was ignored by people at home:

    " As far as the American public was concerned, Korea was an unknown land of little importance... It is also important to note that the Korean War is the first war in which America did not win an ultimate victory, although we did prevent a communist takeover of South Korea. So it was a partial victory, but from America's standpoint, a humiliation by a peasant army, China and North Korea. At the end of the war there was merely a sigh of relief. There were no parades, no show of national pride or support for the veterans. We just came home, and went about building our lives. 'It is over, forget about it, and let's get onto living the good life'—that was the mood of the times. **"**

THE DOMINO THEORY

On April 7, 1954, President Dwight D. Eisenhower used the phrase "domino theory" for the first time. He was talking about Southeast Asia. The theory was that if the French colonial rulers of Vietnam lost control of their colony to communists, then neighboring states would also fall, then their neighbors, and so on—like a row of falling dominoes. The Domino Theory came to dominate U.S. foreign policy.

▼ *Lyndon B. Johnson (center, left) is sworn in as U.S. president for a second term on January 20, 1965. Johnson's foreign policy was shaped by the Domino Theory.*

▼ The black arrows on the map show the feared routes of communist influence.

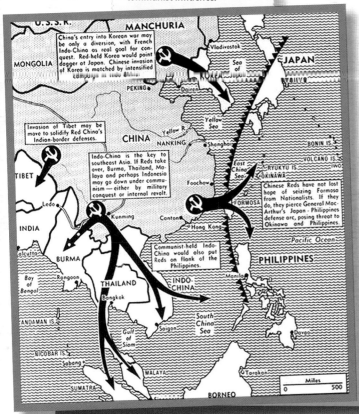

Labels on the map:

U.S.S.R.

MONGOLIA

MANCHURIA

China's entry into Korean war may be only a diversion, with French Indo-China as real goal for conquest. Red-held Korea would point dagger at Japan. Chinese invasion of Korea is matched by intensified campaign in Indo-China.

Vladivostok

Sea of Japan

JAPAN

PEKING

Dairen

KOREA

TOKYO

Invasion of Tibet may be move to solidify Red China's Indian-border defenses.

CHINA

NANKING

Yellow Sea

Yellow R.

Shanghai

BONIN IS.

TIBET

Indo-China is the key to southeast Asia. If Reds take over, Burma, Thailand, Malaya and perhaps Indonesia may go down under communism — either by military conquest or internal revolt.

Foochow

East China Sea

RYUKYU IS.

OKINAWA

VOLCANO IS.

IWO

Ledo

Kunming

Canton

FORMOSA

Chinese Reds have not lost hope of seizing Formosa from Nationalists. If they do, they pierce General MacArthur's Japan - Philippines defense arc, posing threat to Okinawa and Philippines.

INDIA

Calcutta

BURMA

Hong Kong

Pacific Ocean

Communist-held Indo-China would also put Reds on flank of the Philippines.

PHILIPPINES

Bay of Bengal

Rangoon

THAILAND

INDO-CHINA

Manila

ANDAMAN IS.

Bangkok

Gulf of Siam

Saigon

South China Sea

Davao

NICOBAR IS.

Sabang

MALAYA

Tarakan

Miles

0   500

SUMATRA

BORNEO

SOURCE EXPLORED

A U.S. magazine printed this map of Southeast Asia on November 14, 1950, during the Korean War. It showed the possible impact on the region if Korea fell to communism. The black arrows show how communist influence might spread from country to country. In "Red China," Chairman Mao Zedong had declared the communist People's Republic in 1949. Many Americans feared Mao would seek to spread his communist revolution worldwide. As the map shows, according to the Domino Theory, the fall of Korea would be followed by Southeast Asia. It would be only a matter of time before the world's largest democracy, India, was under threat. Similarly, if the Philippines fell, the U.S. military base on Okinawa in Japan might be threatened.

THE BERLIN WALL

After World War II, Berlin, the German capital, was divided. The United States, Britain, and France controlled West Berlin while the Soviets controlled East Berlin. The Soviets tried but failed to defeat the Allies with a blockade in 1948–1949. A decade later, on August 13, 1961, East German soldiers built a barrier across the city to stop East Germans escaping to the West. The wall divided Berlin for twenty-eight years.

▼ Even before the wall was built, the crossings between the U.S. and Soviet sectors of Berlin were guarded by tanks.

▼ *A young man tries to climb the Berlin Wall. The completed barrier included a wall, barbed wire, and open land on either side.*

SOURCE EXPLORED

A young man attempts to climb the Berlin Wall soon after its completion. Before August 1961, more than 3.5 million East Germans (twenty percent of the population) had moved to the West via West Berlin. After the Wall was built, the number fell to a trickle. Escape was not impossible, especially while much of the wall remained little more than a security fence. Around 5,000 people crossed the Wall between 1961 and 1989. At least 171 people were shot trying to cross "the death strip" on either side of the wall.

Ursula Bach was a pregnant young East German who had fled to West Berlin. Her fiancé was still in East Germany. She recalls the radio announcement she heard on August 13, 1961. She never saw her fiancé again:

" It is Sunday August 13, 1961. You are listening to the news on Bavarian Radio. Early this morning in Berlin the border police and members of the operational combat troops started to erect barbed wire and a security fence between the eastern and western sectors of the city. Sixty-nine of the eighty-one border crossings have already been closed. Residents of the GDR [German Democratic Republic, or East Germany] and East Berlin are now only allowed to cross with special permission. The S-Bahn [railroad] is no longer running... **"**

THE CUBAN MISSILE CRISIS

Cuba lies just 90 miles (145 km) from Florida. On January 1, 1959, guerrillas led by Fidel Castro overthrew the Cuban dictator, Fulgencio Batista. Castro was not a communist, but the United States feared for the survival of Cuban-based U.S. businesses if he remained in power and did not back him. The Soviets stepped in to support Castro, who created a communist state in America's backyard. The Soviets used Cuba as a base for its nuclear missiles, leading to an international crisis.

► The Daily News *carries the story of the U.S. blockade of Cuba, with a picture of President John F. Kennedy making the announcement.*

GUANAJAY IRBM LAUNCH SITE 1 WITH
PROBABLE NUCLEAR WARHEAD STORAGE SITE

17 OCTOBER 1962

22-56N 82-39W

GUANAJAY IRBM LAUNCH SITE 1

VEHICLE REVETMENTS

SECURITY FENCE
UNDER CONSTRUCTION

STRUCTURE BEING
EARTH-MOUNDED 114' X 60'

PROB NUCLEAR WARHEAD
STORAGE SITE

CONTROL BUNKER

CONTROL BUNKER

LAUNCH PADS

BATCH PLANT

PRE-FAB CONSTRUCTION
MATERIALS

◄ *This photograph taken from a high-altitude airplane shows the different parts of a missile base under construction in Cuba.*

SOURCE EXPLORED

For thirteen days in October 1962, the world held its breath as it came closer to nuclear war than at any other time. U.S. spy planes took aerial photographs of Soviet nuclear bases being constructed on Cuba. Central Intelligence Agency (CIA) analysts have added labels to the different parts of the base in this photograph. Although some U.S. leaders wanted to strike at the Soviet Union, President John F. Kennedy instead ordered a naval blockade around Cuba to stop the Soviets supplying the sites. He asked the Soviet premier, Nikita Khrushchev, to withdraw the weapons. Everyone was anxious about a possible military confrontation, but finally Khrushchev backed down and the Soviets removed the bases.

BAY OF PIGS

In April 1961, 1,500 Cuban exiles from the United States landed in Cuba to try to overthrow Fidel Castro. The men were trained and armed by the CIA, and were carried in U.S. aircraft and ships. They landed at the Bay of Pigs in southern Cuba but the invasion was a failure. The exiles were quickly defeated and were either captured or killed. The failed invasion caused a rift between the United States and Cuba that lasted until 2014.

ESPIONAGE

The Cold War was an exceptional time for espionage as each side tried to learn about the other. Spies gathered useful information, recruited new agents, and even carried out assassinations. The stakes were high because technology was advancing so rapidly. When the Soviet Union tested its first atom bomb in 1949, the United States assumed a spy must have passed on U.S. atomic plans to the Soviets.

◄ U.S. military observers watch a nuclear test from close range in Nevada in 1955. Many observers later fell sick from the effects of radiation.

SOURCE EXPLORED

This miniaturized camera was used by a Cold War spy to photograph secret documents. Both the United States and the Soviet Union had large espionage networks. The United States formalized espionage in 1947, when the Central Intelligence Agency (CIA) was created to control U.S. espionage and counter-espionage. The CIA aimed to infiltrate the Soviet system to learn about technological advances, military deployments, or political initiatives. The CIA became involved in secret missions in any country where there seemed to be a possible threat to U.S. interests. Some people believed these secret operations fit badly with America's reputation as the defender of the "free world."

▲ The secret services developed cutting-edge technology for espionage, such as this miniature camera.

THE KGB

The Komitet Gosudarstvennoy Bezopasnosti (KGB, or Committee for State Security) was formed in the Soviet Union in 1954. It was a secret police organization in charge of national security. The KGB marked a new development: one organization now controlled the secret police, propaganda, and espionage, as well as suppressing any internal unrest. The KGB became politically very powerful, showing the importance Soviet leaders put on spying.

WAR IN VIETNAM

As early as 1955, the United States had sent advisors to Vietnam in Southeast Asia to help the French colonial rulers resist the threat of communism. When the French abandoned Vietnam and North Vietnam became an independent communist country, U.S. politicians argued that the United States must step in to prevent the spread of communism in Asia. The first U.S. troops arrived in Vietnam in March 1965. The Vietnam War would become the defining event of 1960s America. It became increasingly unpopular at home as U.S. casualties rose.

▼ U.S. Marines land on China Beach near Da Nang, Vietnam, on March 8, 1965. The 3,500 Marines were the first U.S. combat troops to arrive.

◀ *The antiwar feeling behind Paul Szep's nightmarish cartoon from 1967 reflected the growing unpopularity of the war and President Johnson among Americans.*

SOURCE EXPLORED

Paul Michael Szep drew critical cartoons about the Vietnam War for the *Boston Globe* in the 1960s. Here, President Lyndon B. Johnson is haunted by three ghostly skeletons in military helmets. The cartoon summed up the president's dilemma. The "domino theory" argued that the United States should intervene in Vietnam, but the war was unpopular at home. After winning the 1964 presidential election, Johnson authorized Operation Rolling Thunder to bomb North Vietnam and communist positions in South Vietnam. The bombing campaign was supposed to last eight weeks and lasted three years. Johnson did not stand in the 1968 presidential election. Many people believed this was because of the unpopularity of his escalation of the war.

AS THEY SAW IT

66 I have lived, daily and nightly, with the cost of this war ... Throughout this entire, long period, I have been sustained by a single principle: that what we are doing now, in Vietnam, is vital not only to the security of Southeast Asia, but it is vital to the security of every American. 99

—President Lyndon B. Johnson announces his decision not to run for reelection, March 31, 1968.

DEFEAT IN VIETNAM

In 1968, Richard M. Nixon was elected U.S. president on a promise to end the war in Vietnam. In fact he stepped up the fighting and spread it to neighboring Laos and Cambodia, which the communists used as supply routes. Faced by a public outcry, Nixon began a policy of "Vietnamization," in which more and more fighting was taken on by the South Vietnamese Army. The last U.S. troops left Vietnam in 1973, after the loss of some 55,000 U.S. lives.

▲ A communist tank crashes through the gates of the presidential palace in Saigon on April 30, 1975.

DAILY NEWS

GUARDSMEN KILL FOUR STUDENTS

2 of Ohio Riot Dead Are Coeds

Tragedy at Kent State.

◀ *The* Daily News *of May 5, 1970, carried a photograph that became an icon of the antiwar movement.*

FALL OF SAIGON

The fall of Saigon on April 30, 1975, ended the Vietnam War in a victory for communist North Vietnam. The communists had mobilized the whole population in the fight. They absorbed huge casualties to keep the war going, because they guessed that U.S. public opinion would eventually turn against the war. Once U.S. troops left in 1973, the communists massed their forces for the final attack on the South.

SOURCE EXPLORED

Fourteen-year-old Mary Ann Vecchio kneels over the body of Jeffrey Miller just after he was shot dead by the Ohio National Guard on May 4, 1970. The guardsmen killed four students from Kent State University in Ohio when soldiers opened fire on antiwar protests. The photographer, John Filo, won a Pulitzer Prize for his front-page picture, which became a powerful image for the antiwar movement. Some historians believe Nixon withdrew from the Vietnam War because of its growing unpopularity at home. The killings at Kent State turned more Americans against the war and peace marches drew ever larger crowds. In 1971 a march drew 300,000 people. It was clear that the war had to end.

U.S. BACKYARD

Both the United States and the Soviet Union faced problems with their neighbors. Eastern Europeans resented the communist governments the Soviets forced on them. Meanwhile, popular movements in the Caribbean and Central and South America opposed U.S.-backed regimes. The CIA secretly trained and armed rebels to fight anti-American governments there and in countries as far away as Angola and Afghanistan.

▼ *Chilean troops train their weapons on the Presidential Palace in Santiago during the U.S.-backed military coup in September 1973.*

SOURCE EXPLORED

This photograph shows Chile's communist president, Salvador Allende (with glasses), fleeing his palace on September 11, 1973. With secret backing from the CIA, a military coup led by General Pinochet had seized power. The United States had been concerned that Allende would create a Marxist regime in Chile after he was elected president in 1970. The fears grew when Cuba's Fidel Castro visited Chile and Allende oversaw a program of nationalization and collectivization. As the coup took place, Allende gave a farewell speech from the presidential palace and fled. Moments after this photograph was taken, he was dead, probably from shooting himself.

US INTERVENTION

In 1954, the CIA backed a coup in Guatemala to get rid of the left-wing, democratically elected President Jacobo Arbenz Guzman. U.S. involvement in the Caribbean and Central America deepened in the 1980s. After the left-wing Sandinistas took power in Nicaragua in 1979, the CIA trained and backed the right-wing Contras to try to topple the Sandinista government. In 1983, U.S. military forces invaded the island of Grenada, a British dependency, to overthrow its left-wing government.

◄ Salvadore Allende (with glasses) flees the Presidential Palace. He was found dead soon afterward, but no one really knows how he died.

MOON LANDING

The space race between the Americans and the Soviets that had lasted through much of the 1960s ultimately ended in U.S. victory. On July 20, 1969, *Eagle*, *Apollo 11*'s landing craft, finally set down on the surface of the moon. The landing was a U.S. triumph after the early years in space had been dominated by the Soviets, and made astronauts Neil Armstrong and Edwin "Buzz" Aldrin the most famous men in the world. The race for the moon was the most extreme example of the competition between the Soviet Union and the United States in the Cold War.

◀ Apollo 11 *lifts off from Cape Canaveral, Florida, on July 16, 1969. The journey to the moon took three days.*

SOURCE EXPLORED

"Buzz" Aldrin stands beside the Stars and Stripes on the moon on July 20, 1969. The moon landing was a huge propaganda coup for the United States. At least one-fifth of the world's population (around 723 million people) watched live pictures from the moon on TV. The mission had been proposed by President John F. Kennedy in 1961 as a way to stop coming second to the Soviets in the space race. In 1969, it took *Apollo 11* three days from blast-off to reach its destination, where Neil Armstrong became the first man to step on the moon. The U.S. flag was held in place with wire, because there is no wind on the moon to hold it open.

AS THEY SAW IT

" I'm at the foot of the ladder... The surface appears to be very, very fine grained as you get close to it. It's almost like a powder. It's very fine. I'm going to step off the LM (lunar module) now. That's one small step for [a] man, one giant leap for mankind. "

—Neil Armstrong steps onto the moon, July 20, 1969.

NIXON AND CHINA

▲ *President Nixon attends a table tennis tournament in Beijing in February 1972 in acknowledgment of the important role of "ping-pong diplomacy" in U.S.-China relations.*

In February 1972, President Richard M. Nixon made an official visit to China. He was the first U.S. president to visit the communist People's Republic of China. For much of the 1960s, relations between the two countries had been poor, so the visit marked a thaw in hostilities. Nixon intended to separate the two great communist powers, China and the Soviet Union. The Soviets in turn saw China as a threat to their leadership of global communism. For the Chinese and Nixon, however, the visit was a public relations triumph.

SOURCE EXPLORED

President Richard Nixon and his wife Pat (center) stand with their Chinese hosts on the Great Wall of China on a chilly February day in 1972. Their visit was the end result of years of planning by Nixon's Secretary of State, Henry Kissinger, who had already secretly visited Beijing. The U.S. administration wanted closer ties with China, which had fallen out with the Soviet Union. They hoped such ties might also force the Soviet Union into better relations. The images of the trip shown in the United States were the first glimpses most Americans had seen of life in communist China.

PING-PONG

In April 1971, nine table tennis players became the first Americans officially invited to China since the revolution of 1949. U.S. journalists were also invited. The process had begun when U.S. player Glenn Cowan mistakenly boarded the Chinese team bus at an event in Japan. He began talking to the Chinese player Zhuang Zedong, who organized the invitation. This "ping-pong diplomacy" helped to pave the way for Nixon's visit to China.

▲ President Nixon (center, left) and the First Lady (in red) visit the Great Wall of China on February 24, 1972.

33

DÉTENTE

During the early 1970s President Nixon and Soviet leader Leonid Brezhnev took steps to reduce tension between the two superpowers. This process was known by the French word *détente*, meaning "relaxation." Just three months after Nixon's 1972 visit to China, the president flew to Moscow to sign the Strategic Arms Limitation Treaty (SALT I). This limited the number of ballistic missiles both powers could possess. After Nixon left office in 1975, relations between the two powers continued to improve under the new president, Gerald Ford.

▼ *Henry Kissinger (left) and President Gerald Ford (second left) meet President Brezhnev (second right) on a train during talks in Vladivostok in November 1974.*

◀ *Presidents Ford and Brezhnev planned future arms reduction, but the plans were never put into place.*

SOURCE EXPLORED

In this photograph taken on November 24, 1974, President Gerald Ford (left) and Leonid Brezhnev sign a joint communiqué, or statement, after a summit meeting in Vladivostock, Russia. The talks were held as a follow-up to the SALT I agreement, and again the leaders agreed on limitations of missiles and launchers. It was a high point of détente. On his return to the United States, however, Ford was widely condemned for making concessions to the Soviets. In 1976, Ford lost the presidential election to Jimmy Carter and the spirit of détente began to dissolve. A long process of negotiation eventually culminated in SALT II in 1979, but the United States refused to ratify the treaty after the Soviet Union invaded Afghanistan that same year.

MISSILE THREAT

The main purpose of the SALT treaties was to limit the amount of Intercontinental Ballistic Missiles (ICBMs) each side possessed. These missiles could be fired from the Soviet Union at the United States or vice versa. Most of the missiles possessed by each side were not ICBMs, which were not covered. Nevertheless, SALT I was a turning point in the Cold War. It showed both sides were willing to meet face-to-face and negotiate an end to the arms race.

END OF DÉTENTE

In January 1977, Jimmy Carter became president. He wanted to eliminate nuclear weapons, but his foreign policy was unclear and his key advisors had different goals. Secretary of State Cyrus Vance wanted to continue the SALT negotiations but the National Security Advisor, Zbigniew Brzezinski, wanted to establish U.S. superiority over the Soviets. Relations with the Soviets grew worse and hit a low point when the Soviets invaded Afghanistan in 1979.

▶ *Soviet troops guard Afghan prisoners in 1987. Afghan fighters known as* mujahideen *fought against the occupation for a decade.*

SOURCE EXPLORED

President Carter addresses the nation in a TV broadcast on April 25, 1980. He spoke about the disastrous attempt to rescue hostages from the U.S. Embassy in Tehran, Iran. After an Islamic revolution in 1979 saw the U.S.-backed Shah of Iran overthrown, relations between Iran and America collapsed. Iranian students seized the U.S. Embassy on November 4, 1979, and held fifty-two U.S. citizens hostage for 444 days. Carter ordered a hostage rescue mission in April 1980 but some helicopters carrying special forces crashed and the mission was aborted. The failure helped spell the end for Carter's presidency.

▲ *President Carter was widely blamed for his inability to solve the hostage crisis in Iran, and his popularity at home suffered.*

In his State of the Union speech on January 23, 1980, Carter warned the Soviet Union against threatening U.S. interests in what became known as the Carter Doctrine:

" The region now threatened by Soviet troops in Afghanistan is of great strategic importance: it contains more than two-thirds of the world's exportable oil... The Soviet Union is attempting to consolidate a strategic position that poses a grave threat to the free movement of Middle East oil... Let our position be absolutely clear. Any attempt by any outside force to gain control of the Persian Gulf will be regarded as an assault on the vital interests of the United States. And such an assault will be repelled by any means necessary, including military force. "

THE SECOND COLD WAR

Ronald Reagan easily defeated Jimmy Carter in the 1980 presidential election. Reagan believed the Soviet Union still represented a real threat to world peace. In a 1983 speech, he referred to it as an "evil empire." While Reagan ordered a massive U.S. arms build-up, the Soviets had a weak economy and could not afford to compete with the latest weapons technology.

▼ On June 12, 1987, President Ronald Reagan visited Berlin and challenged the Soviets, "Tear down this wall!"

SOURCE EXPLORED

In 1984, an unknown artist imagined a battle in space using the latest "Star Wars" military technology. "Star Wars," named for the popular science-fiction movie, was the nickname given to President Reagan's Strategic Defense Initiative (SDI). Launched on March 23, 1983, the program aimed to intercept nuclear ballistic missile attacks from the Soviet Union. SDI marked a steep escalation in the weaponry and costs of the Cold War. It intended to use space- and ground-based lasers to destroy nuclear missiles in the air. The program was abandoned a few years later because of its cost and the difficulty of getting the new technology to work.

FLIGHT KAL 007

On September 1, 1983, a Soviet SU-15 jet used air-to-air missiles to bring down Korean Airlines Flight 007 as it left Soviet airspace. All 269 crew and passengers died. The Americans condemned the incident as mass murder. The Soviets did not even acknowledge the event until September 6. The shooting down was most likely accidental, but in a climate of fresh distrust it further damaged relations between the United States and the USSR.

◀ An artist's impression of SDI in action: in reality, the technology required for the program was too complex and too expensive to be developed.

PERESTROIKA AND GLASNOST

In March 1985, Mikhail Gorbachev became general secretary of the Soviet Communist Party. His new political thinking would transform both the Soviet Union and its relations with the West. Gorbachev saw that the Soviet Union was heading for economic disaster, so he planned radical reforms. He introduced *perestroika*, a restructuring of the economy, and *glasnost,* an increased openness in politics. To save money, he would cut military spending—which would mean dealing with the United States.

◀ *President Ronald Reagan (left) visits Red Square in central Moscow with Mikhail Gorbachev (right) on May 31, 1988.*

◀ *President Reagan (center) acts as a guide to Gorbachev (left) during a visit to Governor's Island, New York City, on December 7, 1988.*

SOURCE EXPLORED

This photograph, taken on December 7, 1988, shows Mikhail Gorbachev (left) in front of the Statue of Liberty with President Reagan (center) and Vice President George H. W. Bush (right). After Gorbachev became Soviet leader in 1985, he and Reagan met in Iceland in October 1986 and agreed to visit each other's countries. Earlier in his visit to New York, Gorbachev had addressed the United Nations. His announcement that he would reduce and withdraw Soviet troops in East Germany, Hungary, and Czechoslovakia was a clear sign that the Cold War was coming to an end.

AS THEY SAW IT

❝ We were not naive about what might happen. We understood that what was under way was a process of change in the civilization. We knew that, when we pursued the principle of freedom of choice and non-interference in Eastern Europe, we also deprived the West from interfering, from injecting themselves into the processes taking place there. ❞

—Mikhail Gorbachev reflects on the effect of his reforms on Europe in his memoirs, 1995.

END OF THE COLD WAR

▲ Excited Berliners on top of the Berlin Wall watch a man attack the concrete with a pick-ax on November 9, 1989.

As relations between the United States and the Soviet Union improved, it became clear that Gorbachev's reforms were having wider consequences. Eastern European countries such as Poland and Hungary began to rebel against their Soviet-controlled governments. By 1989, the movement was unstoppable. The Soviet Union was breaking up. On November 9, 1989, East German guards watched as Berliners tore down the Berlin Wall, the greatest symbol of the Cold War. The Cold War was over.

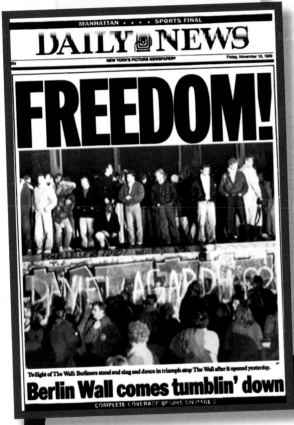

▼ *New York's* Daily News *reports the fall of the Berlin Wall on November 10, 1989.*

AS THEY SAW IT

" For all its risks and uncertainties, the Cold War was characterized by a remarkably stable and predictable set of relations among the great powers. A brief look at the history books will tell us that we cannot say as much about the period leading from the birth of the European nation states up through the outbreak of the Second World War. "

—Lawrence Eagleburger, U.S. Deputy Secretary of State, September 16, 1989

SOURCE EXPLORED

New York City's *Daily News* sums up the triumph that gripped the world with the toppling of the Berlin Wall on November 9, 1989. Since its creation in 1961, the wall had become a powerful symbol of the Cold War. As East and West Germans embraced on top of the wall, it was clear that the Cold War was over. The process had begun with Gorbachev's reforms in the Soviet Union. On August 23, 1989, Hungary opened its borders with Austria. In just three days, more than 13,000 East Germans escaped to the West via Hungary and Austria. On October 18, 1989, the East German head of state, Erich Honecker, resigned. The ban preventing East Germans traveling to the West was lifted. On November 9, 1989, thousands of East Berliners gathered at the Berlin Wall. At 10:30 p.m. the guards let them pass through the wall or climb over it. Berlin was reunited.

TIMELINE

1945	**February 4–11:** At the Yalta Conference, Roosevelt, Churchill, and Joseph Stalin agree the Soviet Union should lead the defeat of Germany, leaving Soviet troops in much of Eastern Europe.
1946	**March 5:** Former British prime minister Winston Churchill decrees that "an 'iron curtain' has descended on Europe."
1947	**March 12:** President Harry S. Truman announces the Truman Doctrine, U.S. support for countries fighting against communism.
	June: The Marshall Plan is set up to provide U.S. aid to the recovering economies of Europe; the Soviet Union and its allies do not join.
1948	**February 25:** A communist takeover seizes power in Czechoslovakia.
	June 24: The Soviets begin an 11-month blockade of Berlin; in response the Allies airlift supplies to the city.
1949	**April 4:** The North Atlantic Treaty Organization (NATO) is formed as an anti-Soviet alliance of Western nations.
	August 29 : Russia tests its first atomic bomb.
	October 1: Communist Mao Zedong takes control of China and establishes the People's Republic of China.
1950	**February:** Senator Joseph McCarthy begins a "witch hunt," seeking out alleged communists in U.S. public life.
	June 24: Backed by the Soviet Union, North Korea invades South Korea, beginning the Korean War.
1953	**July:** The Korean War ends in stalemate.
1954	**March:** The KGB is established in the Soviet Union. The CIA helps overthrow unfriendly regimes in Iran and Guatemala.
1955	**May :** The Soviet Union and its allies form the Warsaw Pact as a response to the formation of NATO.
1956	**June 29:** Soviet tanks suppress demonstrations by workers in Poland.
	October–November: Soviet tanks put down a revolution in Hungary.
1957	**October 4:** The Soviet Union launches the first satellite, Sputnik I.
1959	**January:** Fidel Castro takes power after a revolution in Cuba.
1960	**May:** The Soviet Union reveals that it has shot down a U.S. spy plane.
	November: John F. Kennedy is elected U.S. president.
1961	**April:** A U.S.-backed invasion of Cuba fails to overthrow Castro. **August 13:** East German guards close the Berlin border.

1962	***October:*** *Cuban Missile Crisis.*
1963	***November:*** *Kennedy is assassinated in Dallas, Texas.*
1965	***July:*** *President Johnson announces that he will send 200,000 U.S. troops to Vietnam.*
1968	***August:*** *The Soviet Army crushes a revolt in Czechoslovakia* ***November 5:*** *Richard M. Nixon is elected U.S. president.*
1969	***July 20 :*** *The* Eagle *lands on the moon*
1972	***February:*** *President Richard Nixon visits China* ***July:*** *The Strategic Arms Limitation Treaty (SALT I) is signed.*
1973	***January:*** *A ceasefire comes into force in Vietnam between North Vietnam and U.S. forces.* ***September:*** *A U.S.-backed coup overthrows the government in Chile.*
1975	***April 17:*** *South Vietnam falls to Communist forces.*
1979	***January:*** *The United States establishes diplomatic relations with China.* ***July:*** *The SALT II agreement is signed.* ***November:*** *After the overthrow of the U.S.-backed Shah of Iran, radicals take staff hostage in the U.S. Embassy in Tehran.* ***December:*** *Soviet forces invade Afghanistan.*
1980	***August:*** *The trade union Solidarity protests communist policies in Poland.*
1983	***October:*** *U.S. troops overthrow the government of Grenada.*
1985	*The new Soviet leader, Mikhail Gorbachev begins a campaign of glasnost ("openness") and perestroika ("restructuring").*
1986	***October:*** *President Ronald Reagan and Gorbachev agree to remove intermediate nuclear missiles from Europe.*
1989	***January:*** *Soviet troops withdraw from Afghanistan.* ***June:*** *Poland becomes independent.* ***September:*** *Hungary becomes independent.* ***November 9:*** *The Berlin Wall is demolished; soon East Germany allows unrestricted migration to West Germany.* ***December:*** *Communist governments fall in Czechoslovakia, Bulgaria, and Romania.*

GLOSSARY

Allies The name given to the United States, Britain, France, the Soviet Union, and the countries that fought on their side in World War II.

assassinations Politically motivated murders.

atomic Relating to an atom or other small chemical particle.

ballistic Describes a missile pulled to earth by gravity.

blockade The act of sealing off a place to prevent trade.

boycott To cease buying goods or services from a particular supplier as a protest.

bunker A reinforced underground shelter.

communism A political system based on a lack of private ownership.

coup The sudden, illegal overthrow of a government.

democracy A political system based on elected governments and private property.

deterrent A threat that prevents an enemy from acting.

dictator A ruler who has absolute power over a country.

doctrine A statement about the principles of government policy.

escalation A rapid increase in the intensity of a situation.

espionage The practice of spying or using spies to gain information.

fallout Radioactive particles left in the atmosphere after a nuclear explosion.

guerrillas Irregular soldiers who fight in small groups against larger forces.

hostage Someone detained against their will to achieve a specific goal.

ideologies Systems of ideas and beliefs that form the basis of political and economic policy.

nationalization A process of placing private business under state control.

perestroika A program of economic reform in the Soviet Union.

propaganda Information used to support or criticize a point of view.

puppet states Governments that operate according to the wishes of another country.

ratify To formally approve a treaty.

regime An authoritarian government.

stalemate A contest in which neither side can win.

summit A meeting between heads of government.

superpowers Countries that have global influence.

warhead The explosive part of a missile.

FURTHER INFORMATION

Books

Bryan, Nick. *Nuclear Weapons and the Cold War*. The Library of Weapons of Mass Destruction. New York: Rosen Publishing Group, 2005.

Bodden, Valerie. *The Cold War, Days of Change*. Makato, MN: Creative Education, 2008.

Hillstrom, Kevin. *The Cold War.* Primary Sourcebook. Detriot, MI: Omnigraphics, Inc, 2006.

McNeese, Tim. *The Cold War and Postwar America 1946–1963*.

Discovering U.S. History. New York: Chelsea House Publishers, 2010.

O'Shei, Tim. *Cold War Spies*. Edge Books. Mankato, MN: Capstone Press, 2008.

Roxburgh, Ellis. *John F. Kennedy vs Nikita Khrushchev: Cold War Adversaries*. History's Greatest Rivals. New York: Gareth Stevens Publishing, 2015.

Zuchora-Walske, Christine. *The Berlin Wall*. Essential Events. Minneapolis, MN: Abdo Publishing Company, 2014.

Websites

www.history.com/topics/cold-war
History.com index of Cold War subjects, including many videos.

www.historywiz.com/primarysources/coldwarprimary.html
Extracts from key documents of the Cold War.

www.jfklibrary.org/JFK/JFK-in-History/The-Cold-War.aspx
A Cold War article from the John F. Kennedy Presidential Library.

spartacus-educational.com/ColdWar.htm
Links to many Cold War articles and biographies.

Publisher's note to educators and parents: Our editors have carefully reviewed these websites to ensure that they are suitable for students. Many websites change frequently, however, and we cannot guarantee that a site's future contents will continue to meet our high standards of quality and educational value. Be advised that students should be closely supervised whenever they access the Internet.

INDEX